THE 10 ™

Most Amazing Skyscrapers

Lauren Scremin

Series Editor
Jeffrey D. Wilhelm

D1402933

Much thought, debate, and research went into choosing and ranking the 10 items in each book in this series. We realize that everyone has his or her own opinion of what is most significant, revolutionary, amazing, deadly, and so on. As you read, you may agree with our choices, or you may be surprised — and that's the way it should be!

Franklin Watts®

an imprint of

SCHOLASTIC

www.scholastic.com/librarypublishing

A Rubicon book published in association with Scholastic Inc.

Ru'bicon © 2007 Rubicon Publishing Inc.
www.rubiconpublishing.com

Associate Publishers: Kim Koh, Miriam Bardswich
Project Editor: Amy Land
Editor: Jessica Calleja
Creative Director: Jennifer Drew
Project Manager/Designer: Jeanette MacLean
Senior Graphic Designer: Gabriela Castillo
Graphic Designer: Victoria Cigan

The publisher gratefully acknowledges the following for permission to reprint copyrighted material in this book.

Every reasonable effort has been made to trace the owners of copyrighted material and to make due acknowledgment. Any errors or omissions drawn to our attention will be gladly rectified in future editions.

"Shoe salesman beats 'Spiderman' at own game." This is a partial reprint of a Reuters article. Copyright 2007 Reuters. Reprinted with permission from Reuters. Reuters content is the intellectual property of Reuters or its third party content providers. Any copying, republication or redistribution of Reuters content is expressly prohibited without the prior written consent of Reuters. Reuters shall not be liable for any errors or delays in content, or for any actions taken in reliance thereon. Reuters and the Reuters Sphere Logo are registered trademarks of the Reuters group of companies around the world. For additional information about Reuters content and services, please visit Reuters website at www.reuters.com" License # REU-GC6076

"Skyscraper that may cause earthquakes," by Kate Ravilious, December 2, 2005 Copyright Gaurdian News & Media Ltd 2005

Cover image: Petronas Towers – Shutterstock

Library and Archives Canada Cataloguing in Publication

Scremin, Lauren
      The 10 most amazing skyscrapers/Lauren Scremin.

Includes index.
978-1-55448-480-5

      1. Readers (Elementary) 2. Readers—Skyscrapers. I. Title.
II. Title: Ten most amazing skyscrapers.

PE1117.S429 2007   428.6   C2007-900538-1

1 2 3 4 5 6 7 8 9 10   10   16 15 14 13 12 11 10 09 08 07

Printed in Singapore

Contents

6

18

38

ABOVE AND BEYOND

Skyscraper — the word conjures up the image of a tall, tall building soaring into the skies and piercing the clouds. These structures, created to increase the use of limited land in crowded cities, are marvels of design and engineering. The earliest skyscrapers were built in the late 19th century in Chicago and New York. Today, skyscrapers fill the skyline in major cities around the world. They have even become symbols of prestige, with cities competing against each other for the most amazing structure. The newest skyscrapers are being built with more style and flair than ever before, using methods that were once thought to be beyond anyone's wildest imaginations.

If you wanted to build the greatest skyscraper in the world, what characteristics do you think it must have? Let's face it — a skyscraper that seems to touch the clouds would be amazing enough. But don't you think the most amazing should have something extra to brag about? What if it had a bridge way up in the sky, or was strong enough to stand up against the worst typhoon imaginable? How about some entertainment, like a giant indoor gym, state-of-the-art theater, or even an underwater restaurant? If you think these ideas are far-fetched, read on!

In this book, we present what we think are the 10 most amazing skyscrapers today. Some are luxurious, most are built to last, almost all are super-tall, and a few have unique designs. As you read about these splendid structures, ask yourself:

IF YOU HAD TO AWARD A PRIZE TO THE MOST AMAZING SKYSCRAPER IN THE WORLD, WHICH ONE WOULD YOU CHOOSE?

10 SEARS TOWER

HEIGHT: 1,450 feet

LOCATION: Chicago, Illinois, United States

CONSTRUCTION: 1970 to 1973

WOW FACTOR: A tower of tinted glass, this massive skyscraper was the world's tallest for 25 years and was built using revolutionary construction methods.

In late 1969, Sears, Roebuck and Company commissioned the building of the Sears Tower — a massive skyscraper that would soon become the world's tallest structure. Not only was the tower a record-breaking engineering achievement, but it was built with construction methods that had never been used before.

Finished in early 1973, the tower held the "tallest" title for 25 years. And even though it was surpassed in height in 1998 by the Petronas Towers in Kuala Lumpur, it hasn't lost its fame. A jewel in the Chicago skyline, it attracts millions of visitors every year who want to get a bird's-eye view of the city. So, if you think a skyscraper has to be new to be great, think again! The Sears Tower still fascinates with its unique design, revolutionary construction, and amazing height. As one of the modern era's first great skyscrapers, it ranks #10 on our list ...

SEARS TOWER

LOOKING GOOD

The Sears Tower stands at 1,450 feet tall and is 110 stories high. It has four different sections and is designed so that each gradually tapers in — so the taller the tower gets, the thinner it becomes. It is built using steel with a black aluminum exterior and bronze-tinted glass. Every section has a thick black band at the top.

BUILT TO LAST

The tower was designed by architect Bruce Graham and structural engineer Fazlur R. Khan. Their challenge was to create a building large enough to fit all of the employees from Sears, Roebuck and Company, a huge retailer at the time. Khan actually came up with the building's "bundled tube" concept. This was a brand-new idea first used on the Sears Tower. The tower would be supported by a system of exterior beams and columns. This would create a "hollow tube" that could withstand the strong winds of Chicago. All of the tower's steel was pre-made, with almost all of the welding done off-site.

CLAIM TO FAME

The Sears Tower was officially the world's tallest structure for 25 years. Each year, over 1.5 million people visit the Skydeck Pavilion to get the best view of Chicago. This sky-high lookout measures 1,353 feet above ground and was added to the tower in 1985. To get to the top, tourists can ride one of the 76 single-deck or 14 double-deck elevators. The ride is worth it because on a clear day you can see four states from the lookout — Michigan, Indiana, Illinois, and Wisconsin. On a windy day, visitors can even feel the tower swaying!

? After the 9/11 attacks, the Skydeck was actually closed for several weeks for security. How would you feel having to work in a very tall building after that event?

? After the tower was completed, Sears never did use all of the office space. By 1995, Sears had moved out completely. Do you think it should still be called the Sears Tower? Explain your answer.

Quick Fact

In 1982, two TV antennae were added to the top of the tower, making its total height 1,706 feet. In 2000, one antenna was raised another 20 feet to improve reception.

The Expert Says ...

"The Sears Tower skyscraper in downtown Chicago is constructed as a 'bundled tube' structure. ... The tower is really more like nine straws tied together, and each tube gains strength and support from the others pressing against it."

— Dr. Thomas Mical, Carleton University, School of Architecture

UNDER CONSTRUCTION

Read this fact chart and learn more about the construction of the Sears Tower.

The Sky's the Limit!

It was May 3,1973, and a crowd of more than 1,000 people gathered around the Sears Tower to celebrate the day when the last beam was raised. The beam was signed by more than 12,000 construction workers, Sears employees, and Chicago residents. The building wouldn't be officially finished until 1974, but in the construction world "topping-out" is the most exciting part of the process, almost like a climber reaching the top of a mountain.

Bumps in the Road

As the building kept getting taller, it became impossible for construction workers to trudge all the way back down to street level for coffee and lunch breaks. How do you think they solved this problem? They installed portable kitchens on the 33rd and 66th floors.

Blown Over

Another major problem for construction workers was the wind. The workers had to climb ropes and balance on six-inch-wide beams to do their job. But at more than 1,300 feet in the air, the wind was so strong that they could barely stand without getting knocked over. Since there was no real solution to the high winds, this was the only problem that caused delays. They don't call Chicago the "Windy City" for nothing.

Quick Fact

In 1999, French stunt climber Alain "Spiderman" Robert scaled the tower with his bare hands and feet. Fog near the top of the building made the glass and steel very slippery and hard to climb, but he got to the top safely!

Take Note

This skyscraper is #10 for having held the world record for tallest building for 25 years, which is a pretty long time! What is even more amazing is that the Sears Tower was built in 1973, without the help of today's modern technology!
• Do you think there is anything that can be done to update the Sears Tower or do you think it should stay just the way it was built back in 1973? Explain why or why not.

5   3   2   1

9 30 ST. MARY AXE

HEIGHT: 590 feet

LOCATION: London, England

CONSTRUCTION: 2001 to 2004

WOW FACTOR: Not only was it built to look like a giant pickle, but it is one of the most environmentally friendly buildings in London.

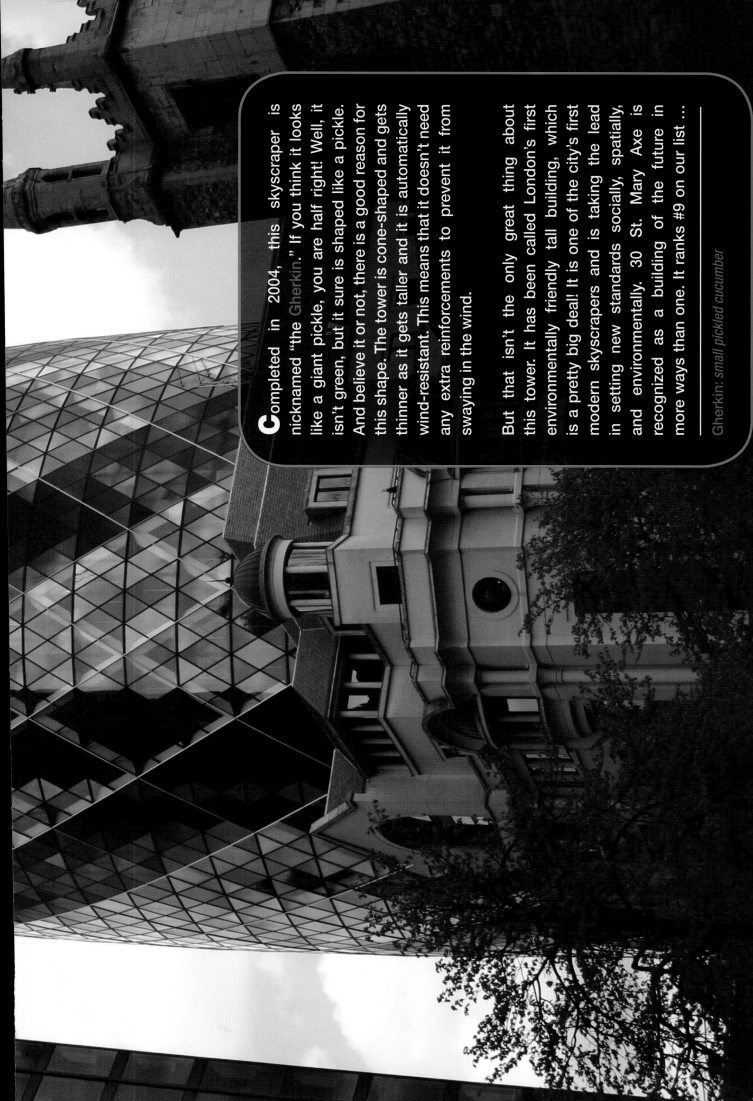

Completed in 2004, this skyscraper is nicknamed "the Gherkin." If you think it looks like a giant pickle, you are half right! Well, it isn't green, but it sure is shaped like a pickle. And believe it or not, there is a good reason for this shape. The tower is cone-shaped and gets thinner as it gets taller and it is automatically wind-resistant. This means that it doesn't need any extra reinforcements to prevent it from swaying in the wind.

But that isn't the only great thing about this tower. It has been called London's first environmentally friendly tall building, which is a pretty big deal! It is one of the city's first modern skyscrapers and is taking the lead in setting new standards socially, spatially, and environmentally. 30 St. Mary Axe is recognized as a building of the future in more ways than one. It ranks #9 on our list…

Gherkin: *small pickled cucumber*

30 ST. MARY AXE

LOOKING GOOD

At first glance, this 40-story skyscraper looks like a giant glass rocket preparing for takeoff. At 590 feet high, the daring architecture and unique cone shape sure make it stand out. Built for both beauty and function, its shape reduces the wind turbulence around it. The shiny glass panels on the outside are shaped like diamonds. It has this twisty design because each floor is rotated five degrees from the one below. But looks can be deceiving — even though it seems curvy, there is only one piece of rounded glass on the entire tower — the lens cap at the top!

BUILT TO LAST

After a bomb damaged a historical building originally on this site, plans were put into place for a reconstruction. The architects at Foster and Partners designed a new building that would really be noticeable. They came up with the circular plan that would be known as 30 St. Mary Axe — a building that widens as it rises from the ground and then tapers toward the very top. The 40 floors of the building are different sizes because of the exterior shape and the floor plan that is laid out like a flower with six petals.

CLAIM TO FAME

As London's first environmentally friendly tall building, 30 St. Mary Axe is truly a skyscraper of the future. Not only is it an office building, but there are private dining rooms on the 38th floor, a restaurant on the 39th floor, and a lookout on the 40th floor that has a 360-degree view of London. There is even a public plaza inside with shops and restaurants. This unique skyscraper has won over 10 awards, including "the most admired new building in the world" in 2005!

30 St. Mary Axe has been both admired and criticized. It has won many awards, but in June 2006 it was nominated as one of the five ugliest buildings in London. Why do you think some people might not like its design? What do you think of it?

It's easy to spot the unique shape of 30 St. Mary Axe in this view of London.

BUILT SMART

BUILT GREEN

This fact chart explains just how environmentally friendly this building is.

LIGHT & VENTILATION

The building's design makes good use of daylight, so it reduces the amount of time that artificial light is needed. Sensors make sure lights are not on when they aren't needed. Gaps in the floors create shafts that work as a ventilation system for the whole tower, making it cooler in the summer and warmer in the winter. This means less use of air-conditioning and heating.

TRANSPORTATION

Full public transportation around the site makes it easier not to use private cars. There are also three times more bicycle spaces than in regular buildings, encouraging the use of this clean way of transportation.

EXTERNAL ENVELOPE

The building has a double layer on the outside that reduces heating and cooling needs. Blinds inside the hollow spaces between the double layer capture solar heat, so that it can be used or rejected, all depending on what is needed at the specific time.

BUILDING SYSTEMS

The building uses gas, which is one of the cleanest fuels. Instead of using a central energy system for the entire building, ventilation is supplied on a floor-by-floor basis, to better match supply and demand.

The Expert Says...

"30 St. Mary Axe sets a precedent for skyscrapers of the future in terms of minimizing energy consumption. Great skyscrapers of tomorrow should not only compete with height, but should keep stride with environmentally friendly technological advancements.

— Dr. Mohamed Elkady, Ph.D., structural engineer

precedent: *example for others to follow*

Take Note

30 St. Mary Axe takes the #9 spot. It is newer than the Sears Tower, so it had the advantage of more modern technologies. It is also one of the most environmentally friendly skyscrapers in the world. Not many skyscrapers are built to save precious energy resources.

• Why do you think it's important for skyscrapers to be built in an environmentally friendly way? What are some of the things you can do to help save the environment?

5   4   3   2   1

8 KINGDOM CENTRE

HEIGHT: 990 feet

LOCATION: Riyadh, Saudi Arabia

CONSTRUCTION: 1999 to 2002

WOW FACTOR: A graceful, sleek, and futuristic structure that looks like a larger-than-life bottle opener

Imagine seeing a flat skyline for most of your life and then suddenly — *POP!* — a 41-floor skyscraper appears to break up the otherwise empty sky. This was the experience of residents of Riyadh, Saudi Arabia. Up until 2002, they had only seen buildings that didn't go higher than a few stories.

Well, they aren't the first people to get a skyscraper built on their turf, but they certainly are the first to get a tower that looks like this one. That's because this isn't just any building — it's a skyscraper that looks like a huge, shiny bottle opener! The next time you need to open a hundred-foot-tall bottle, look no further than Saudi Arabia. As a landmark skyscraper in the Middle East, the Kingdom Centre ranks #8 on our list ...

KINGDOM CENTRE

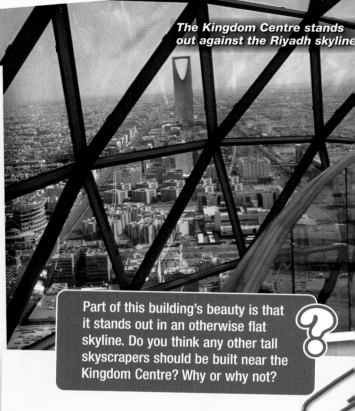

LOOKING GOOD

The Kingdom Centre stands almost 1,000 feet tall. It has a long oval floor plan and ends in a parabolic curve creating a giant U-shape. Connecting the tips of the U-shape is a skybridge that is 213 feet long. This creates the illusion of a window opening up into the sky. The outside of the building is very shiny and is covered in different shades of gray, all as a result of the different materials used (including concrete, granite, brushed aluminum, silver, and reflective glass).

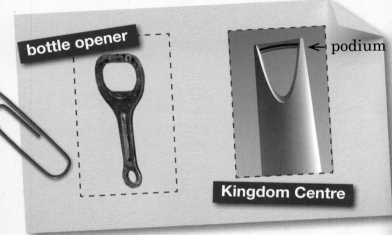

bottle opener

← podium

Kingdom Centre

BUILT TO LAST

Kingdom Centre was built for Prince Alwaleed of Saudia Arabia. He held a competition among 100 of the world's greatest architects to decide who would design this building. American architectural firm Ellerbe Becket won the competition, thanks to their design. The design uses two podiums on either side with a tower in the center. The center tower acts like a concrete core for stability with a superstructure of concrete columns made from thick floor slabs. The flat slabs are eight inches thick with beams that link the outside columns to the concrete core.

parabolic: *arched shape*
superstructure: *part of the building built above something else*

Part of this building's beauty is that it stands out in an otherwise flat skyline. Do you think any other tall skyscrapers should be built near the Kingdom Centre? Why or why not?

CLAIM TO FAME

The Kingdom Centre is the tallest skyscraper in Saudi Arabia and the 25th tallest in the world.

Believe it or not, the empty space is its coolest structural feature — the developer called it a "necklace" for the city of Riyadh. The building houses a sports club, wedding and banquet hall, luxury apartments, and a three-floor shopping mall. Even though the building is a very modern structure, it still respects Saudi Arabia's traditional customs. It is equipped with prayer rooms and a special floor called the "Ladies Kingdom" that is for women only.

Quick Fact

Residents in Riyadh are proud of this building because it shows that Saudi Arabia can compete in the global economy.

10   9   **8**   7

LESS IS More

So, how does having a big hole at the top of a building help to make it more stable? This report explains it.

Think about what would happen if you stuck a long stick in the sand and tried to blow it over. Would you blow toward the stick's base or its tip? What if you could blow really, really hard? Now, imagine the Kingdom Centre without the opening at the top. All of the wind forces that once went through the opening would be pushing on the building itself, at the very top where it is the most vulnerable.

So, without the opening, the architects would have had to include some safety feature to strengthen its wind resistance. When you think about it, the opening at the top of the Kingdom Centre is a pure stroke of genius — it creates a tunnel for the wind to flow through, making the entire tower harder to blow over. It makes the building look unique and it adds structural strength to the entire skyscraper!

Quick Fact

Design matters! Even light fixtures in the parking lot and wastebaskets in the building have the same shape as the tower!

The Expert Says...

" In addition to the obvious architectural benefit, the large U-shaped opening at the top of the building allows for a decrease in the wind load acting on the building. So basically the building can be designed using the same total wind force as a shorter building, but still have a taller, more impressive elevation.

— Paulino Hipolito, B.Eng., structural engineer

Take Note

The Kingdom Centre has many different qualities that put it at #8 on our list. It looks like a giant bottle opener that soars up into the sky. It has a cool skybridge and it respects local customs.
- Why do you think it is important for major buildings to accommodate traditional customs? If a giant skyscraper was built in your city, what local customs would you like to incorporate into its design?

5   4   3   2   1

7 OSAKA WORLD TRADE CENTER

HEIGHT: 1,722 feet

LOCATION: Osaka, Japan

CONSTRUCTION: 1995

WOW FACTOR: Not only does it offer visitors a trip to the cosmos, but it actually has a pyramid on its roof!

Completed in 1995, the Osaka World Trade Center (WTC) is part of a larger complex of buildings on the Osaka waterfront called Cosmos Square. What do you think of when you hear the word cosmos? If you picture stars, galaxies, and planets, then you have the right idea.

Compared to others on our list, this skyscraper is literally out of this world! Most of the building's interior is designed to represent the solar system. Everything from the lights, to the floors, to the doors, to the walls is meant to remind visitors of outer space. And if an indoor solar system isn't enough to get your attention, how about a huge pyramid that sits right on top! As one of the great structures along Osaka's skyline, this skyscraper takes the #7 spot on our list ...

OSAKA WORLD TRADE CENTER

View of Osaka, Japan, at night

LOOKING GOOD

It looks like a tall rectangle that is covered in shiny reflective glass. There are triangular supports at the base, which match the famous inverted pyramid on the building's roof. This three-dimensional figure is actually an observation deck called "Top of the Bay." It provides a 360-degree view of the city. The inside was designed by a famous Japanese architectural firm called Mancini Duffy. They designed it to look like the universe or cosmos.

As a focal point, the elevator tower rises from a pool and waterfall. The marble floor has a design of the constellations. Planetary orbit rings are created with different shades of gray marble.

---

inverted: *turned upside down*
focal point: *central point of focus; place that draws attention*

? Can you think of anything the architects could have done to the outside of the tower to follow the cosmos theme?

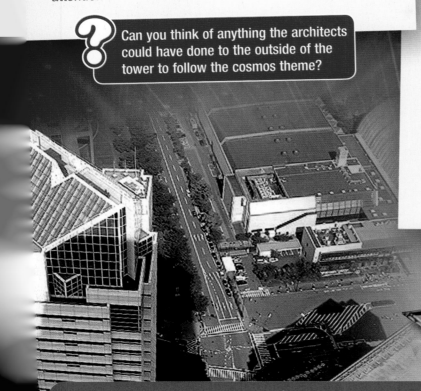

BUILT TO LAST

The tower was built with state-of-the-art technology. It uses high-tech smoke systems and computerized vibration controls to help survive fires and earthquakes. It also uses a special air-conditioning system to help protect the environment.

CLAIM TO FAME

The Osaka WTC is the second-tallest building in all of Japan. This tower was designed mostly for office use, but it also includes a restaurant, private club, retail stores, and even an all-weather park. If you were lucky enough to ride up to the top of this tower, you would do it in style. The elevator can travel 52 floors in just 80 seconds and the elevator walls are actually transparent. This means passengers inside can see the view as they ride up higher and higher! As the tallest building in the region, the Osaka WTC is also used for communication. It is home to one of Osaka's biggest media centers and many business branches around the world.

OSAKA WTC: BY THE NUMBERS

Check out this **chart** to run down some of the building's standout numbers.

55	number of total floors above ground
32,290	total area of the entrance hall in square feet
215,278	total area of the building's site in square feet — that's just over the combined size of four football fields!
1,614,586	combined area of all the floors in square feet
200,000	number of people the building can hold at one time

The Expert Says...

"Designing the inverted pyramid on the top of the building would not have been easy due to its large surface area and very small base. Keeping in mind that typhoon winds are common in Japan, it is similar to a person facing into a very strong wind with their feet side by side rather than spread apart for stability."

— Dave Scremin, B.Eng., structural engineer

Take Note

We think the Osaka World Trade Center beats out the Kingdom Centre to take #7. It looks cool both on the outside and on the inside! The giant upside-down pyramid is definitely as unusual as the bottle opener, but what sets this skyscraper apart is its galaxy theme. Any building that lets you feel like you are walking among the stars and planets is definitely out of this world.

• Do you think this tower's greatest feature is its exterior or the interior cosmos theme? How important is interior design when ranking a skyscraper?

5   4   3   2   1

6 TURNING TORSO

HEIGHT: 623 Feet

LOCATION: Malmö, Sweden

CONSTRUCTION: 2001 to 2005

WOW FACTOR: Putting a "twist" on the common skyscraper, this building is based on the turning torso of a human body.

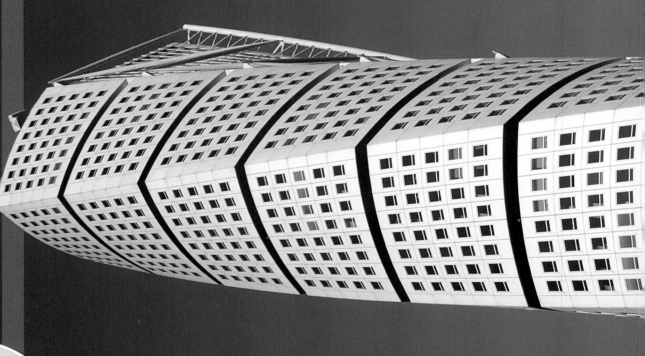

The Turning Torso is definitely not your typical building. It has an unusual name and an unusual design to match! If you think it looks like it should be in an art gallery, you are totally right. That's because this skyscraper with a twist is actually modeled after a famous sculpture!

But something else makes this 54-story building stand out. Unlike most of the skyscrapers on our list, the Turning Torso is not only used as an office building, but it also contains 149 luxury apartments. This unusual skyscraper is becoming so popular that it's quickly turning into one of Sweden's most visited tourist attractions and has already inspired copycats. As the first of its kind, this twisty art-inspired tower ranks #6 on our list ...

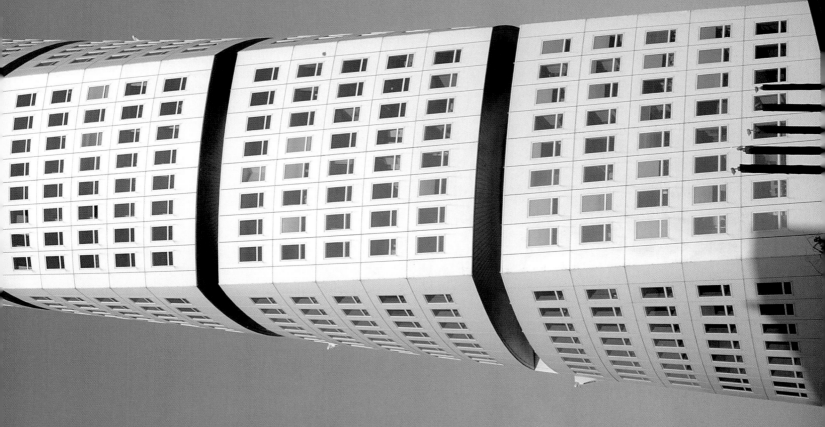

TURNING TORSO

LOOKING GOOD

This building is constructed from nine cubes of white marble stacked on top of one another. Instead of being stacked straight up, each cube is twisted 11 degrees from the one below. The top cube ends up being twisted 90 degrees from the bottom one, making the building look like a twisting human spine. Because of the twisty shape, the apartments inside have unusually shaped rooms. Instead of being rectangular, they are shaped like pieces of pizza. The windows are shaped like parallelograms.

Parallelogram

Architect Santiago Calatrava

BUILT TO LAST

The core of the building is shaped like a concrete pipe. Inside the core are elevator shafts and staircases. Slabs shaped like giant slices of a pie are attached to the core. These slabs are fitted together to create an entire floor. Each floor is then twisted to create the unique turning look of the building. The outside of the building is covered in curved aluminum panels. The building's frame is made from vertical white steel tubes attached to the tower with horizontal tubes.

Quick Fact

In 2005, the Turning Torso won the Emporis Skyscraper Award by the largest margin in history!

CLAIM TO FAME

The Turning Torso is the first twisting skyscraper of its kind and has already inspired copies such as the Infinity Tower in Dubai. Unlike other skyscrapers on our list, this building only has two floors of office space and the rest are apartments. The building also houses the Turning Torso Gallery. This is an area that has many unique attractions, shops, and restaurants, and features the best in Swedish design.

Quick Fact

Because of the curving shape, it was impossible to use hoists during construction. The main core elevators were used to lift materials and were built in stages as the structure rose. Gusts of wind at the site also delayed work on the steel skeleton by 150 days.

SANTIAGO CALATRAVA

– A profile of the architect and artist

The Expert Says...

" Calculating wind loads on the Turning Torso is beyond conventional methods. The demand of continuously changing angles can only be accomplished with relatively new developed computer modeling applications. "

— Lee Levoir, structural engineer

The design for the Turning Torso is based on a famous sculpture by Spanish architect Santiago Calatrava (San-ti-a-go Ka-le-tra-va) called *Twisting Torso*. The sculpture is a white marble piece based on the form of a twisting human being. Johnny Örbäck (Oor-baack), former head of the Malmö co-op housing association, saw the sculpture in 1999 and asked Calatrava to design a building using the same concept.

? Do you think that Calatrava succeeded in using the same concept? In what ways is the building similar to the *Twisting Torso*?

Inspired by the movements of animals and humans, Calatrava creates his work with a sculptor's eye. By mixing the free forms of art with strict geometry and modern technologies, he crosses boundaries to design unique and fascinating buildings. He once called the shape of this building "helicoidal," which is a technical term for spiral. To better explain his concept, Calatrava drew a human body resembling a tennis player in the middle of a swing. He then sketched a tree trunk and finally, a perfect spiral. He did this to explain what he had in mind for the Turning Torso — a tower that rose naturally resembling forms in nature.

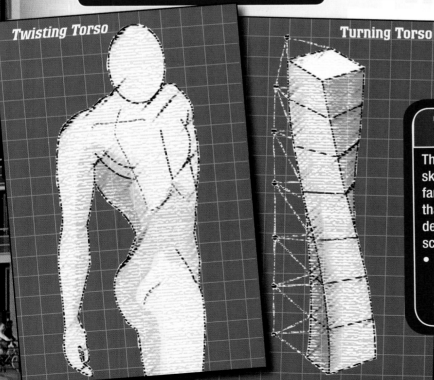

Twisting Torso

Turning Torso

Take Note

The Turning Torso rises to take the #6 spot. We think this skyscraper has the most interesting shape and name so far. The building itself lives up to its name, with a design that is unique. Part of the Turning Torso's greatness definitely comes from the fact that it is modeled after a sculpture of a human being.
- How important do you think it is for buildings to reflect nature? If we judged skyscrapers on exterior looks and artistic influence, how would you rank the Turning Torso compared to the other buildings so far?

5   4   3   2   1

EMPIRE STATE BUILDING

HEIGHT: 1,250 feet

LOCATION: New York City, New York, United States

CONSTRUCTION: 1930 to 1931

WOW FACTOR: Built during the Great Depression, this skyscraper went up in record time and revolutionized the construction of tall buildings.

The Empire State Building may be the oldest skyscraper on our list, but if you think its age makes it less amazing than the others, think again! Not only was it the tallest in the world for 41 years, but it was built in record time rising about four-and-a-half floors a week.

And even though it isn't the tallest anymore, it is still known for some very important firsts. It was the first building to have more than 100 floors and was the first built with a 360-degree lookout. It shot to fame first in 1933, and then later again in 2005, when a giant ape we all know as King Kong climbed up its side. A skyscraper that has truly stood the test of time, the Empire State Building ranks #5 on our list ...

EMPIRE STATE BUILDING

The building's spire at the very top was supposed to be a landing spot for Zeppelin airships, but after some tests this turned out to be too dangerous. The spire was kept because it adds height to the tower.

LOOKING GOOD

The world-famous Empire State Building is a 102-story Art Deco-style skyscraper. It weighs 363,760 tons and has 6,500 windows! Its exterior is limestone and granite and is built with several setbacks. The huge, decorative spire at the very top, combined with thousands of vertical windows, makes the tower look taller. The lobby is a five-floor masterpiece made with granite, marble, and brushed stainless steel. It is decorated with enormous bronze medallions to honor the craftspeople who helped build the tower. Inside the lobby is a metal mosaic that features the building as the center of the universe.

BUILT TO LAST

William Lamb, an architect from the firm Shreve, Lamb & Harmon, designed the Empire State Building. From the time construction began, the building's steel frame rose four-and-a-half floors per week. To speed up the building time, the posts, beams, windows, and window frames were made in factories and put together on-site!

mosaic: *art made from pieces of stone or glass*

CLAIM TO FAME

Built during the Great Depression of the 1930s, the Empire State Building was (and still is) a supreme example of American creativity and strength. It was the first building to have a 360-degree lookout, which became a popular tourist spot. It has since become a symbol of the city and has been featured in artwork, on album covers, on television shows, and in movies. One of the unique features about the building is its floodlights that come on at night, in colors to match different holidays and special events.

The architect said he based most of his design for the Empire State Building on the clean lines of a simple pencil. How do you think the building resembles this writing tool?

Quick Fact

During the Depression, jobs were hard to come by. Most of the tower went unrented for many years because of this.

The Expert Says...

The Empire State Building is one of the tallest skyscrapers in the world. But what is so amazing is the fact that this skyscraper was designed and constructed without the aid of computers or any modern technology.

— David Scremin, B.Eng., structural engineer

9   8   7   6

A STAR IS BORN

The Empire State Building is probably New York's best-known skyscraper and has grown to become a recognized symbol of the city. Over the years, it has played a starring role in many famous films. This list runs down some of its most legendary appearances …

An Affair to Remember

Sleepless in Seattle

⭐ AN AFFAIR TO REMEMBER — 1957

Handsome Nicky Ferrante and beautiful nightclub singer Terry McKay fall in love on a cruise from Europe to New York. They decide to reunite six months later at the Empire State Building. But before Terry can get there, tragedy strikes and Nicky is left waiting for his one true love at the famous landmark.

⭐ SLEEPLESS IN SEATTLE — 1993

Sam Baldwin has just lost his wife to cancer. One evening, Sam calls into a national radio show and is heard by thousands of women across the nation, including Annie Reed. Annie, although engaged to be married, can't rest until she meets Sam. She eventually does that at the top of the Empire State Building.

⭐ KING KONG — 1933, 2005

Probably the skyscraper's greatest cameo. Kong is a giant ape who is captured and taken from his home on Skull Island to New York to be exhibited. He escapes and climbs the Empire State Building, where he is shot and killed by airplanes.

Take Note

The Empire State Building takes the #5 spot. But even though it is the oldest, it is the most famous skyscraper on our list. It held the height record for decades, had the world's first 360-degree lookout, and was built in record time.
• Do you think this skyscraper should get extra credit for doing a lot of things first? Explain.

5

King Kong, 2005

3   2   1

4 PETRONAS TOWERS

HEIGHT: 1,483 feet

LOCATION: Kuala Lumpur, Malaysia

CONSTRUCTION: 1995 to 1998

WOW FACTOR: With twin towers connected by an awesome skybridge, these buildings have become a Malaysian icon.

The Petronas Towers are great for more than one reason — mainly because there are two of them! When these twin towers were completed in 1998, they stole the title of world's tallest building from the Sears Tower (#10 on our list). For the first time ever, an Asian skyscraper held these bragging rights. While the Petronas Towers have since been surpassed in height, they are still the tallest twin towers in the world — not to mention that they have a super-high skybridge connecting them. Imagine how much fun it would be to walk across that bridge way up in the sky and get a bird's-eye view of the world below.

But the Petronas Towers are unique for more than just their height. They are the only skyscrapers on our list that weren't built with steel. They have become a major status symbol for Malaysia. If these things aren't enough to convince you of their greatness, turn the page to find why we ranked them #4 on our list...

PETRONAS TOWERS

Petronas Towers

LOOKING GOOD

If you think you're seeing double — think again. The Petronas Towers are not one, but two identical 88-story buildings that were designed by architect César Pelli. They actually look like cylinders with jagged edges. The outside is made from glass and aluminum. The tower's floor plan is based on simple Islamic geometric shapes of two interlocking squares creating the shape of eight-pointed stars. The two towers are joined by a skybridge that is located between the 41st and 42nd floors. The bridge is 190 feet long, and weighs 909 tons!

BUILT TO LAST

The Petronas Towers were built on the world's deepest foundations — 394 feet — and required massive amounts of concrete. In an unusual move, a different construction company was hired for each of the towers to compete against each other. Eventually, the builders of tower two won the race, even though they started a month after tower one. Because the builders couldn't import enough steel, the towers were built using super high-strength reinforced concrete. This concrete gives double the sway reduction against wind, but makes the building twice as heavy on its foundation.

CLAIM TO FAME

The Petronas Towers were built in the middle of Asia's economic boom and have become a status symbol for Malaysia. They have been featured in films, on television, in books, and even in video games. And not only are they used as office buildings, but they have shopping and entertainment facilities and house the Petronas Concert Hall — home to the Malaysian Philharmonic Orchestra. This massive concert hall has 864 seats and state-of-the-art acoustics.

acoustics: *sound quality*

? The Petronas Towers proved that Kuala Lumpur was becoming a modern city that could compete economically with bigger North American and European cities. How do you think they show this?

Quick Fact

The towers have a total of 76 elevators and 58 of these are double-deck. This means that there are two standing-room elevators, one on top of the other. It takes only 90 seconds to get from the basement parking lot to the top of each tower using these elevators.

10 9 8 7 6

BUILDING THE SKYBRIDGE

One of the most difficult feats during the Petronas Towers' construction was the placement of the two-floor skybridge. Read this account to learn how they did it.

The skybridge was fully assembled in South Korea and was then taken apart and shipped to Kuala Lumpur in 493 separate pieces. It was built on the ground and then hoisted up using a giant crane. After it was lifted into position, the legs were swung down into place and connected underneath the bridge. The entire process took about 30 hours.

The design of the skybridge was complicated because the bridge had to be strong enough to withstand the swaying movements of both buildings. The final solution was an inverted V that supports it in the center. The bridge also could not be rigidly fixed to the buildings since they move independently. To fix this problem, it rests on what are called "sliding supports." These allow the bridge to move sideways and back and forth, but keep it from falling or lifting up.

The skybridge is important because it links the two skylobby levels between towers. This allows for easy access to meeting rooms, dining rooms, and prayer rooms. Most importantly, because the bridge is smoke and fireproof, it can be used as an exit path in case of emergency.

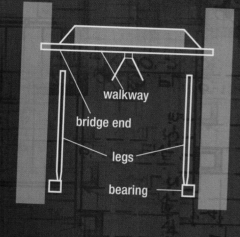

walkway
bridge end
legs
bearing

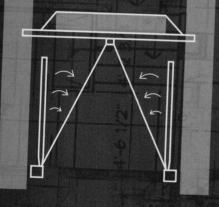

The Expert Says...

" I tried to express what I thought were the essences of Malaysia, its richness in culture and its extraordinary vision for the future. "

— César Pelli, architect

essences: *characteristics*

Take Note

Unlike the previous selections on our list, there are two Petronas Towers. For a short time, these towers were the highest in the world. But that's not why we ranked them at #4 above the Empire State Building. The sky-high skybridge is their claim to fame. It is not only unique, but it is also helpful to people working inside.
- The Petronas Towers are not the only buildings on our list with a skybridge. Compare their skybridge with others in this book. What do you think makes their skybridge stand out?

5   **4**   3   2   1

3 JIN MAO TOWER

HEIGHT: 1,380 feet

LOCATION: Shanghai, China

CONSTRUCTION: 1994 to 1998

WOW FACTOR: This tower perfectly blends traditional Chinese and modern design. Plus, it boasts the highest swimming pool and hotel in the world!

Since it was completed in 1998, the Jin Mao Tower has been recognized as the tallest building in China and has become an international symbol for Shanghai. It's no surprise because many cultural symbols were incorporated into its design. This includes a pagoda and the number eight (considered lucky by many Chinese people) woven throughout the entire structure.

This tower was built to withstand the major typhoons and earthquakes that are common to the area. To add to the challenge, builders had to make up for the fact that it's built on soft soil – definitely not the sturdiest spot for a massive skyscraper. So, how do you think they did it? Read on to learn more about the Jin Mao Tower and why it ranks #3 on our list ...

pagoda: *Asian temple*

JIN MAO TOWER

LOOKING GOOD

Chicago architect Adrian D. Smith designed this skyscraper to show a perfect balance between traditional Chinese architecture and modern design. Glass, stainless steel, and granite were used for the outside — an interlaced design was then created using aluminum pipes. The building's design revolves around the number eight.

interlaced: *spun or twisted together; intertwined*

? If you were designing a skyscraper for your country, what symbols, numbers, or pictures would you include?

BUILT TO LAST

Because the tower was built on soft soil, the foundation rests on over 1,000 steel piles driven almost 276 feet deep. These piles are capped by concrete slabs that are 13 feet thick, with a basement wall that is three feet thick and 118 feet high. The swimming pool on the 57th floor helps to support the building against typhoons. The weight of the water works like a damper, helping the tower to withstand high winds.

CLAIM TO FAME

Feel like going for a dip? The Jin Mao Tower's 57th-floor pool is the world's highest! This tower also houses the highest hotel in the world, the Shanghai Grand Hyatt. The hotel takes up floors 53 to 87, with an atrium that soars to a height of 377 feet. The atrium's corridors and staircases are lined to create a perfect spiral with a sunny, circular opening at the top.

piles: *poles driven into the earth to carry the structural load*
damper: *object that reduces vibration*

The Expert Says...

> What is most impressive about this skyscraper is that it is designed to withstand earthquakes up to seven on the Richter Scale and winds up to 200 kilometers [125 miles] an hour, which can easily occur in this area of the world. The top of the building can move laterally 75 centimeters [30 inches] under these types of forces.

— Lee Levoir, structural engineer

laterally: *sideways*

Quick Fact

On top of the hotel is the largest and highest observation deck in China called the Skywalk. This indoor observation deck can hold over 1,000 people. You can either look over Shanghai or look down into the hotel's famous spiral atrium.

10   9   8   7   6

SHOE SALESMAN BEATS "SPIDERMAN" AT OWN GAME

An article from Reuters, February 27, 2001

Shanghai — The French "spiderman," the daredevil famous for clambering up the Eiffel Tower and the Empire State Building, has been upstaged in China by a shoe salesman.

Alain Robert walked away from Shanghai after he decided that shimmying up the 88-story Jin Mao Tower — China's tallest building — was too risky.

Enter Han Qizhi, a 31-year-old shoe salesman who just happened to be walking past the popular landmark and was "struck by a rash impulse," according to one state media report.

When security guards weren't looking, he launched himself on the skyscraper and proceeded to clamber — bare-handed and dressed in ordinary street clothes and shoes — up a steel grid that sheathes the building, state media reported.

Han hoped his death-defying stunt in high winds, near-zero temperatures, and swirling fog might help promote his shoe

business in the central Chinese city of Hefei. A trim, athletic-looking man, he had never climbed before. ...

By the time Han was grabbed by policemen in a window-cleaners' moveable perch just short of the summit, his hands were raw and bleeding. ...

Looking up at Jin Mao Tower

French "spiderman" Alain Robert also climbed the Sears Tower. Why do you think these stunts are so risky?

Take Note

It doesn't have the double towers or skybridge like the Petronas Towers, but the Jin Mao Tower's amazing design and ingenious use of a swimming pool as a damper to steady the building in high winds make it more special at #3.

- Compare the Jin Mao Tower's ability to withstand typhoons and quakes with the Petronas Towers. If a natural disaster were to strike, which skyscraper would you feel safest in and why?

5   4   **3**   2   1

2 TAIPEI 101

HEIGHT: 1,667 feet

LOCATION: Taipei, Taiwan

CONSTRUCTION: 1997 to 2003

WOW FACTOR: Not only is the Taipei 101 the tallest skyscraper on our list, but it houses the world's largest damper ball to support the building against typhoons and earthquakes.

If being tall is a part of being great, then Taipei 101 is a definite candidate — this skyscraper rises nearly half a mile! The only thing trickier than building such a tall tower is building it in a region prone to earthquakes and typhoons. This massive skyscraper gets hit by winds that can reach speeds of almost 100 miles an hour — that's faster than the speed of most cars! To top things off, it was built only 650 feet away from a major fault line! Luckily, the people who designed it knew a thing or two about how to protect it against nature's assaults.

But the plot thickens! Some scientists worry that this 772,000-ton skyscraper is so heavy that it may have reopened the ancient fault line. In a nutshell, the tower may cause future earthquakes! With all of these problems, it's a miracle that Taipei 101 is still standing. It is truly an engineering marvel that has defied all odds. That's why it's the #2 greatest pick on our list...

TAIPEI 101

LOOKING GOOD

Taipei 101 got its name because it has 101 floors above ground. It is supposed to look like a giant stalk of bamboo. The building is divided into sections that symbolize gold bricks used by ancient Chinese royalty as money. Like the Jin Mao Tower, the number eight was used as a design symbol — there are eight different sections, each with eight floors. Near the base there are four circles on each side of the building that represent ancient Chinese coins.

? During the building's construction, five people were killed when an earthquake shook two cranes loose. What other natural disasters would make it hard to build a skyscraper? How do you think builders should protect against such unexpected events?

Quick Fact

Taipei 101 was no bargain — it cost around $1.7 billion to build! The giant damper ball alone cost about $4 million!

The 805-ton damper ball

BUILT TO LAST

Taipei wasn't an obvious spot for a 1,667-foot building. Not only is the city known for typhoons, but it sits on the most seismically active area on Earth. Because of this, architect C.Y. Lee hung a 805-ton steel ball with a 16-foot-wide diameter from the 92nd floor. It prevents the tower from swaying during earthquakes and typhoons by transferring wind and other vibrations to an underground spring system. Taipei 101 was also built with a flexible frame to absorb quakes. Twenty-four vertical columns add support, a steel web adds flexibility, and trusses connect the columns to the building's core.

CLAIM TO FAME

Besides its height and its gigantic damper ball to protect it from typhoons and earthquakes, this building boasts the world's fastest elevators. It takes only 39 seconds to whoosh up to the observatory, at a speed of 39 miles an hour. There are 61 of these high-speed, double-deck elevators, so there's no waiting in line here!

---

seismically: *relating to vibrations from earthquakes*
trusses: *framework of beams creating a rigid support*

The Expert Says...

"The purpose of the tuned mass damper ball is to limit the motion of the structure when it is subjected to a particular force, such as wind or earthquakes. This system is similar to the shocks in a car. Without the shock absorption the building would continue swaying back and forth and the occupants on the upper floors would get motion sickness."

— Dr. Mohamed Elkady, Ph.D., structural engineer

10   9   8   7   6

Skyscraper that may cause EARTHQUAKES

By Kate Ravilious
Article from *The Guardian*, December 2, 2005

Taipei 101 is a building with a lot to boast about. Standing 508 meters [1,667 feet] high, it is the world's tallest. And at 700 000 tonnes, [772,000 tons] it must be among the heaviest.

But the sheer size of the Taiwan skyscraper has raised unexpected concerns that may have far-reaching implications for the construction of other buildings and mega structures. Taipei 101 is thought to have triggered two recent earthquakes ...

According to the geologist Cheng Hong Lin, from the National Taiwan Normal University, the stress from the skyscraper may have reopened an ancient earthquake fault. ...

Before the construction of Taipei 101, the Taipei basin was a very stable area with no active earthquake faults at the surface. ...

However, once Taipei 101 started to rise from the ground, things changed. The number of earthquakes increased to around two micro-earthquakes per year ...

Using the construction information, Dr. Lin has calculated how much pressure Taipei 101 exerts on the ground. The weight of steel and concrete came to more than 700 000 tonnes [772,000 tons].

Quick Fact

Remember daredevil climber Alain Robert who scaled the Sears Tower? He was so worried about the high winds in Taipei that he used a safety rope to make the four-hour climb to the top of Taipei 101!

This is spread over an area of 15 081 square meters, [3.73 acres] meaning that it exerts a huge pressure ... on the ground below. "The construction of Taipei 101 is totally different to many other high-rise buildings because it used hybrid structures made of both concrete and steel, to give it added protection from earthquakes and fire. Therefore it has a huge vertical loading on its foundation," says Dr. Lin.

And it is this exceptional downward stress that Dr. Lin thinks may have caused the extra earthquakes. ...

basin: *natural dip in land, often with a lake at the bottom of it*

? Do you think it was a wise idea to build such a high tower in a city that is known for natural disasters? Do you think the builders did enough to protect Taipei 101 in case of an emergency? Why or why not?

Take Note

Taipei 101 slips into the #2 spot. Like the Jin Mao Tower, Taipei 101 blends traditional culture with modern design. The big difference is its height — Taipei 101 is taller than any of the other skyscrapers in this book. Plus, the architect created the world's largest damper ball to help the building withstand earthquakes and typhoons.
• What buildings do you know combine traditional culture with modern design?

5   4   3   **2**   1

BURJ AL ARAB

1

HEIGHT: 1,053 feet

LOCATION: Dubai, United Arab Emirates

CONSTRUCTION: 1994 to 1999

WOW FACTOR: Rated the world's first seven-star hotel, the Burj Al Arab is built on an artificial island that is connected to the mainland by a private bridge.

The Burj Al Arab may not be the tallest, oldest, or most famous building on our list, but it gets top scores for being the most distinctive. Unlike any other building Dubai has ever seen, the Burj is a futuristic architectural marvel towering over the Persian Gulf.

For a start, it doesn't even look like a building — it looks more like a huge sailboat. To create the illusion that the hotel was floating in the ocean, it was built on an artificial island that was specially created for it! The island is 920 feet from the coast and connects to the mainland by only one curving road. And unlike any of the other skyscrapers on our list, the Burj Al Arab is an exclusive seven-star hotel, the only one in the world. Decorated with gold leaf, marble, granite, and crystal, it has been described as "pure, sheer luxury." That is why it is one of the most expensive hotels in the world and attracts only high rollers who can afford thousands of dollars for a suite.

With a surprise around every corner, a trip to the Burj Al Arab is truly out of this world. If the incredible design doesn't amaze you, the mind-blowing activities will. Visitors can choose between taking a submarine ride to an underwater restaurant or whizzing up an elevator to eat in the sky!

Turn the page to find out exactly why the Burj Al Arab earns the #1 top spot on our list ...

BURJ AL ARAB

Quick Fact

Out of respect for local culture and religious beliefs, many of the Burj Al Arab's facilities are for women or men only. So, there are specific times when only one of the two genders is allowed into a certain area.

LOOKING GOOD

The Burj Al Arab is a stark white building designed to look like the billowing sail of a *dhow*, which is a type of Arabian vessel. The frame is made from three giant steel pylons — the two outside pylons are curved and the middle one is vertical. Near the top is a helipad and on the other side of the hotel, supported by a cantilever over the ocean, is a restaurant. The outer wall of the atrium that faces the beach is made of a woven, Teflon-coated fiberglass cloth. This Teflon shield protects the building from the desert's sun and heat. At night, the outside lights change every 30 minutes and vary from white to multicolored.

cantilever: *beam anchored at one end and projecting into space*

? Not many people can afford to stay at the Burj Al Arab, but for an entrance fee day visitors can eat in the restaurants. Why do you think it is important to let the "average person" visit?

The Burj Al Arab's luxurious atrium

Hotel lobby

BUILT TO LAST

The Burj Al Arab was designed by architect Tom Wright for His Royal Highness Sheik Mohammed. Wright designed the hotel to look like a ship that was approaching, but never reaching, the land. To achieve this effect, the hotel was built on an artificial island! Piles had to be drilled and rooted 130 feet into the seafloor to support the island's weight. It took three years to build the island and just under three years to put up the hotel.

CLAIM TO FAME

Not only is the Burj Al Arab the world's tallest hotel, but it is also the most luxurious. The hotel has 202 duplex suites. The Royal Suite is the most expensive and costs approximately $30,000 for just one night! It has a private dining room, movie theater, and revolving bed. The hotel also has an underwater seafood restaurant. Diners are driven to the restaurant in a 12-seater submarine. Along the way they are treated to a shark-filled aquarium that runs along the walls. Now that's a sight to see!

The Expert Says...

"It is amazing that even though no existing support system was initially in place, the building solidly rests on 250 piles which go to a depth of about 50 metres [165 feet] below the sea.

— Saleem Moledina, B.Eng., structural engineer

AFRAID OF Heights?

Try to imagine what it would be like to play tennis in the sky. This firsthand account explains exactly what tennis legend Andre Agassi and world number one player Roger Federer did in February 2005. They took the game to new heights when the Burj Al Arab converted its rooftop helipad into a tennis court — the pros had a skytop game over 650 feet above sea level. The hotel's grass helipad has a surface area of 4,467 square feet with only a safety net for protection, so the two had to be very careful about getting too close to the edge.

Take Note

The Burj Al Arab doesn't even come close to the height of Taipei 101 or many of the earlier rankings on our list, but we feel it deserves the #1 spot because of its unique structural design, out-of-this-world entertainment features, and state-of-the-art technology.

• Do you think these features make up for the building's lower height? Would you rank the Burj al Arab the most amazing skyscraper in this book? Why?

❝When you first get over how high you are and start playing it's an absolute joy ...❞
— Andre Agassi

5   4   3   2   **1**

We Thought …

Here are the criteria we used in ranking the 10 most amazing skyscrapers.

The skyscraper:
- Is especially tall
- Is built with innovative building methods and materials
- Has a unique design
- Has cool, never-before-seen features
- Respects local customs and surroundings
- Is able to withstand forces of nature
- Has an interesting interior to match its unique exterior